Bitter Chovy

Esther Lee

BookLeaf Publishing

India | USA | UK

Presentation by *BookLeaf Publishing*

Web: www.bookleafpub.com

E-mail: info@bookleafpub.com

ISBN:9789358315752

First edition 2024

she who twists the Knave

the first of November, a timely hail
strikes and trickles as shotted blood.
callous North winds call to her in war cries—
she sings back an elegy for the end.

she trudges, prances, and titters,
knowing that the Haunter lies in wait.
she pauses, plods, and listens
to furtive waters who peruse her fitful steps.

in her halt, her palms cup the blood-soaked earth
who cannot distinguish the white frigidity
and—invisibly freezes as do her eartips.
her quivering eyes crack into a dreadful smile.

the unspoken Knave who tiptoes on her mouth
is swallowed by the demises and awakenings of
Time.

chiaroscuro

none, none, none
trickle on your feet.
none, none, none
crawl up to your head
or whisper of your beloved's musings.

no caress nor kiss could outlast
the profound comfort that entices
both heavenly light and peripheral darkness.

with no option to resist,
your heart is lost and so is mine.

wondrous winter

cold goes well with cold; an iced
coffee with milk in hand, a ready morning.
a short farewell to the irksome girl; out
of the increasing crowd we move. not
underdressed but not warm; we open
into another crowd—but lo! look above!
a flurry of soulless leaves pretending to be crows
like the same flurry of snowflakes pretending
to be dander about ten minutes ago.
in a moment, you see a winter specter
and i concede, dissipating.

bean sprouts

mother told me,
go clean the bean sprouts
with your dad as usual.
cleaning bean sprouts meant
i take off the ends of the sprouts
and throw away the bad stems.
my hands would craft
small yet grown sprouts,
snapping ends with a
slight *crack!*
and rid dirty skins
in the dafty plastic.

today's bean sprout job
was not the same.
my father took away
the pizza-stained dishes
we had for dinner and started
picking the beans
by my side.
we chat about the
news, small topics,
until he brings up
a revelation.

you would be fine if
i stayed in any place
other than new york, right?
he peered into my
eyes but i cast them
down to my hands.
if i went to tacoma
or los angeles, you
would be able to handle it, right?

i watched my fingers
wrinkle and
smear themselves in the
natural oil, whilst sniffing
the musty odor of
these bean sprouts.
i did not dare speak,
kept my mouth shut,
for if i did, i would
shed a tear or more.

he kept talking. i,
with my head down,
focused on the sprouts,
these sprouts, clutching
and snapping their
ends as quickly as
i could. no matter
how much oil covered

my fingers or how much
of their smell was
absorbed into my
hands and mind,
i did what i had
to do.

i only had to focus
on finishing this
massive pile of
bean sprouts
because if i did,
i would see the
bottom of the
stack.

bitter chovy

when there are no more nails to spare,
this mouth of mine gets bored.
when my chattering teeth are bare,
i tug upon the chovies on the fraying cord.

fried and dried, dipped in a flavorful red,
their bitterness gives my mouth a bed.

highest point

igniting the rain, the morning shower
does not clean away the bird's sorrows.
it whispers that the only way to rid them
is to revel and burn.

again, the glittering pavement guides
the little bird. the cold moon accompanies
him this time and shares the secret
of the waters—only for the bird to scoff
and return to his nest, shivering.

unholiness

disturbed is the silence
of elusive rage, where
seduction is cast into chests.

disturbed is the blood
of the forgiving, who
stalked the proud with chimes.

the isolation of threads,
untangled from humanity,
reconfigured into soot.

it thrives.

the intricacy of a paradise,
long lost in shadows,
refracted through none.

it dies.

rearranged are all
the angels with
shattered horns.
none trustworthy,
none merciful.

beyond consciousness,
beyond integrity, reality
is in ponderance
of new delusion.

lost image

photographed
lying still
black mass all around
pleasant aromas waft to his closed lids

cold hands grasp the Word
wrinkled and dry are they
i want to warm them

makeup covers his face
to hide away his weariness
to mask the draught state

i miss him

my grandfather

paperlife

a mysterious crumpled paper flings
in front of me. i watch it unfold in front of you.

no, i only live to see how exactly
it unfolds. no absurd change, no
more crumpling. still wrinkly.

if i were like the brave ones,
maybe pencil marks would appear on every fold;
or would it flatten itself out? (would that be
boring?)
or perhaps these unique folds are what make us,
us.
but i can't life a pen on this paper.

it is not that this wrinkly paper
is useless, but i. helpless
compost i turn into as i become one
with landfill, not soulful nature.

a day of my youth (and bad luck)

a day of bad luck is
when you can't find the shirt you want to wear
nor your sneakers that are not as cruddy as the
others,
when you are right on time for school
but are told to get a late pass,
when you realize wore your socks the wrong
way
but can't change it since your feet are already
stinky.

a day of bad luck is
when people only talk to you for answers to the
homework
and you refuse to say, making them glance at
you,
when your group in English class is unorganized
and is still inconsiderate towards you,
when you quickly run out of stamina during gym
because of high expectations the teacher puts
onto your unathletic body.

a day of bad luck is
when you get looks from your biology teacher

for pointing at a picture of him on the door,
which you've actually never seen before,
when the people who you thought were friends
don't greet you when you did,
when you don't get a good score on your Latin
test
and hear the shrill shriek of the girl you don't
like.

a day of bad luck is
when you don't understand what's going on in
math
because you could not communicate with the
others,
when you yell like an idiot in the hallways
earning looks from your peers,
when the friend you love is being pulled
away from someone else.

a day of bad luck is
when the bus doesn't plan to come
in the next thirty minutes
so you walk that twenty-minute walk back
home,
drenched in sweat from the summer heat,
when your father complains about
you taking long in the shower,
when you're stressed but proceed to do
nothing at all, because of the

bad luck fate decided to give you
today.

hypothermia faker

i thought that i liked being cold,
the cold hands i bragged to everyone in my
youth.
but now i strive to keep myself warm
habitually found myself layering,
stuffing hands into cuffs
(to rather enjoy the cold, not be it).

i liked my cold self. i was happier
but blind. now i am in constant demise
of myself but crave menial warmth.
nonchalant i am but i reside in silence
and yearn amidst nothing, this lukewarm winter.

170124

the present is illimitable,
my heart is made out of magnesium.
why is it friday?
the stars are smoky grey,
my imaginations are mystique,
and melancholy is a juxtaposition.
there is eloquent piano music
in the midst of the slicing of spicy rice cakes.
don't defenestrate on a cloudy day
in royal january.

nightmare

the morning of october seventeen,
i woke up to the sound of the door slamming.
it was my sister who had gotten into an
argument with my mother last night.
my mother yelled "hey" and tried to get my
sister back in.
that's when i realized my mother prepared her
lunch.
i smelled the steamed carrots, the food in my
slumber.
eyes still closed, i sighed.
several curses were uttered when my mother
returned.
the constant calamity of the dishes
irked my untimely sleep.
but i could feel her tears from afar.

back into my dreams i went.

media

inhibited by the old and young,
who take comfort in these kitsches
that are garnished by the tongue.

midsummer is rich with lush leaves
that beg endlessly to be picked.
winter is abundant in fur sleeves
that seek for warmth to be bricked.

those engines go back and forth
restlessly, erratically, undirected
to locales that are not of fine worth,
especially to an unprejudiced fool.

but white screens keep them in,
fixing corners they've never been.

tiny joys

ten days of twenty-three cradled
in a bookcase of flowers waiting
to wilt. perhaps, they only stand
until i forget—then will they droop.

but they bloom notoriously in their corner,
their veins entwining me in their luster,
immovable. i continue to revel in them
until their stories end and more flowers appear.

mbti list

21

a fun record, a light topic
while i precisely guess strangers,
now acquaintances and friends.
i took this from two, started
with twelve, currently thirty-four,
and counting. what use are they?
indeed, inaccurate and silly they are but

they are names i wish to etch on cloth,
their thought processes i wish to understand,
a form of love, a keepsake.

sfumato

if not today or centuries ago, i wonder
how i would view Earth's delicacies.
will they be offered to me on plates of ants
or in the ink of burning lanterns? will she wait
for me to inch closer? truly, i do not dwell
on these what-ifs but if i could not trace
out your every arm hair or read your lips,
how could i call myself a painter of this world?

trompe l'oleil

every Nothing wants to trick the paths
of adventurers walking cloudless cities.
the Nothings gnaw into ears then souls
and scavenge eyes once ahold of memories,
leaving no reality behind but a state
of terror and lunacy defined as
nothing.